St. Maurice And The Theban Legion, By The Author Of 'good King Wenceslas'

ST. MAURICE

AND

THE THEBAN LEGION.

ST. MAURICE

AND

THE THEBAN LEGION.

By the Author of " Good King Wenceslas."

PUBLISHED UNDER THE DIRECTION OF
THE TRACT COMMITTEE.

LONDON:
SOCIETY FOR PROMOTING CHRISTIAN KNOWLEDGE.
SOLD AT THE DEPOSITORIES:
77 GREAT QUEEN STREET, LINCOLN'S INN FIELDS;
4 ROYAL EXCHANGE; 48 PICCADILLY;
AND BY ALL BOOKSELLERS.

CLARENDON PRESS, OXFORD.

FOR THE SOCIETY FOR PROMOTING CHRISTIAN KNOWLEDGE.

ST. MAURICE

AND

THE THEBAN LEGION.

"UNCLE MAX, did you ever wish to be a soldier?"

Hugh lay on the sofa by the drawing-room window, for the leg he had broken in his fall down the church tower still needed plenty of rest, and he was only able to hobble about now and then with a crutch. Uncle Max was writing letters at a table near him, and answered, without looking up,

"I have been a soldier for the last twenty-seven years."

"A soldier! Uncle Max!" exclaimed

Mabel, jumping up from the low stool on which she sat in the window, to peer at her uncle across the sofa.

"Well, Mabel, have you any objection?"

"But you are a clergyman! and twenty-seven years—why—"

"Do you think I was not born then, Puss? Well I was—let me see—this day twenty-seven years I was just three weeks old!"

Mabel's eyes grew rounder and rounder as she stared at this mysterious uncle, who was always giving her fresh food for wonder.

"But, Uncle Max, if you were only three weeks old how *could* you be a soldier?"

"Ask Hugh," said Uncle Max, and went on writing his letters.

"I don't believe Hugh knows any more than I do," said Mabel, rather discontentedly. "I wish you would tell me what you mean."

"Don't teaze so, Mab!" interrupted Hugh. "Can't you see Uncle Max is busy?"

"Well, you spoke to him first—and I don't see why you should stop me directly *I* do."

"Very well, Miss!" said Hugh, with an air of lofty displeasure. "Then I shall not tell you what I was going to!"

"Come, come, you two recruits! you seem to be forgetting your own commission in quarrelling over mine! If you don't look out you will find yourselves in the enemy's camp in no time!"

And Uncle Max looked up for a moment with the brilliant smile which the children always thought lighted his face like a flash of sunshine. It was the only sunshine there was that afternoon, for after long drought the welcome rain had come, and was pattering through the leaves and filling the room with the delicious cool fragrance of fresh earth, borne in through the half-open window. Mabel looked more than ever puzzled at this last remark, and Hugh coloured, and stared out upon the rain pools on the lawn, and

the dripping boughs of the great cedar, with
a somewhat discomfited expression.

"Mab," said Uncle Max, "run up to my
room, and fetch me my Prayer-Book. Now's
your time, Hugh!" he added, cheerily, as the
little girl left the room. "Go in at him
roundly, that old giant Pride! Turn him
out before Mabel comes back, or he'll hand-
cuff you so that you won't be able to find
the place I want you to show her in the
Baptismal Office."

Hugh made no answer—he stared harder
than ever at the old cedar—and when Mabel
returned, and by her uncle's desire put the
book into his hands, he boggled over it more
than seemed necessary before finding the
right place; but finally he held it out to his
little sister, and said, gently,

"This is what Uncle Max means, Mab—
at least I think so."

"Read it out, Puss," said Uncle Max,
whose pen was again flying over sheet after
sheet of paper—"and then I shall know if

Hugh is right." And Mabel read slowly and reverently—

"'We receive this child into the Congregation of Christ's flock, and do sign him with the sign of the Cross, in token that hereafter he shall not be ashamed to confess the faith of Christ Crucified, and manfully to fight under His banner, against sin, the world, and the devil; and to continue Christ's faithful soldier and servant unto his life's end.'"

"Did you mean that, Uncle Max?" she asked softly, after a little pause.

"Yes, dear."

"But that was not what Hugh meant, was it?"

"Never mind, Mab, don't disturb Uncle Max any more."

"I can talk now," said Uncle Max, smiling. "I have broken the backs of my letters for to-day. So you don't think I have answered Hugh yet, little one? Nor do I. Well, Hugh, I don't know that I ever particularly wished to wear a red coat and charge at the cannon's mouth, as you are always panting to do, ferocious elf that you are! But there was a time when I was constantly reading about soldiers, and battles, and fatal wounds, and what not! and pestering my friends to tell me all sorts of horrible stories of war and bloodshed. So you see there is some hope of your settling down into a peaceable citizen like myself some day, in spite of all your taste for warfare now!"

"I don't want to!" said Hugh, stoutly. "I do hope papa will let me be a soldier! Do you think he will?"

"If when you are old enough you seem to be fitted for it, I have no doubt he will; but you must wait a while and see what is pointed out to you as the *right* thing, my lad."

"But, Uncle Max, isn't it wicked to go to war?" asked Mabel. "And aren't soldiers always bad men?"

"It is not wrong to go to war in a good

cause—to uphold what is right, and put
down what is wrong—when it cannot be
done by peaceful means. And as to soldiers
being necessarily bad men—why, at that rate
you do away with all the warrior Saints of
Christendom, besides the noble host of
Christian Soldiers who have of late fought
the more bravely as knowing that their life
was in God's hands, not their enemies'!"

"Who do you mean by the 'Warrior
Saints,' Uncle Max?"

"Did you never hear of St. Sebastian, or
of St. Maurice, or of our own St. George?
Soldiers, every one of them—yet content to
die without striking a blow in self-defence,
rather than turn traitor to the Captain Whom
they had been pledged to serve long before
they entered the army of an earthly ruler!"

"I thought 'St. George and the Dragon'
was a fairy tale!" said Mabel. "I'm sure
I've read it somewhere."

"I daresay some people would tell you
that all the lives of the Saints are no more

to be believed than fairy tales!" said Uncle
Max, smiling. "And certainly the legend of
St. George of Cappadocia always seems to
me more a parable than a history."

"I know about him and St. Sebastian,"
remarked Hugh; "but I never heard of
St. Maurice. Who was he, Uncle Max?"

"Wait till I have directed these letters,
and I will come and tell you about him,"
was the welcome reply; at which both
the children set up a shout of triumph, and
Mabel flew to wheel what she considered a
"comfy-chair" close to the sofa; and then
fidgeted about, first on one foot and then
on the other, quite unable to keep still, till
her uncle was ready to take the seat prepared for him, and give her the one she
coveted on his knee.

"Now, Uncle Max," she said, "please
begin at the very beginning, and make it a
nice long story! because, you see, we can't
get out at all this afternoon."

"But *I* must, Puss! so it is as well that

I cannot make it a very long story if I would."

"Must you really go out in all this rain? Can't you wait till to-morrow?"

"Do you think I should be a faithful soldier if I only went on my commander's errands in fine weather, little one? How about St. Paul's words — 'Thou therefore *endure hardness*, as a good soldier of Jesus Christ [1]'? But I must begin my story, or we shall be hurried at the end.

· "It was the month of September, long, long ago—in the year of our Lord 286. The Emperor Diocletian had not long before divided the enormous Roman Empire into four parts, under the government of himself and three other princes; keeping the eastern portion in his own hands— while his fellow-emperor, Maximian, who shared his title of 'Augustus,' ruled Italy and Africa; and of the other two (who were called the 'Cæsars') Galerius governed

[1] 2 St. Tim. ii. 3.

Germany; and Constantius (the father of
the first Christian emperor, Constantine,)
Gaul (or France), Spain, and Britain. The
people in Gaul seem to have been rather
unruly just then, and the *Bagaudæ*, an important tribe among them, having broken
out into open rebellion against the Romans
—the Emperor Maximian marched towards
Gaul with a large army, vowing the destruction of every Christian he found there!"

"But why, Uncle Max? What had the
poor Christians done?"

"I have no doubt they were accused to
him as having been at the bottom of this
insurrection; because it was, you know, the
interest of the pagans and their idolatrous
priests to cast as much blame of all kinds
as possible on the Christians, of whom they
were getting very jealous—for there were
Christians by that time in all parts of the
Empire, and amongst all ranks, and it made
the false priests furious to see noble churches
to the One True God rising on all sides,

and becoming more and more thronged with
zealous worshippers, and beautified with
costly offerings ; while *their* temples to
Venus, and Mars, and Diana, were less
sought, and they themselves less honoured
and bribed year by year. So they were
always on the watch to provoke the
governors against their Christian subjects ;
and the surest way to do this was to per-
suade them that Christianity made people
disloyal, and was at the bottom of all the
rebellions and disturbances which troubled
the Empire."

"Was that the beginning of the persecution of Diocletian?" asked Hugh.

"Yes. That persecution was the last
great stand° made by the false religion
against the true. Diocletian would probably never have interfered with the
Christians, if the priests had not worked on
his superstitious terrors—though Galerius
was their open enemy, and Maximian was
sometimes their friend and sometimes their

c

foe, according to his ideas of their useful-
ness to the state.

" But the time I am speaking of now was
seventeen years before the terrible Edict of
Diocletian was issued; and it was only here
and there that some occasional panic or ill-
feeling on the part of a governor found vent
in a sudden outburst of fury against the
Christians immediately under his eye.

" Well, the Emperor Maximian marched
against the Bagaudæ, and, to strengthen his
forces, Diocletian sent from his own army
in the East what we should call now a
' crack regiment,' named the *Theban Legion*,
because it had been raised in the *Thebaide*,
the district in Africa which we now call
Upper Egypt, of which that huge city of
Thebes was the capital."

" But I thought Thebes was in Greece,
Uncle Max?"

" *One* Thebes was, Puss, the Thebes
founded by Cadmus; but this was an older
and a greater Thebes—a city which was in

its greatest glory 1600 years before the birth of our Lord—that is, about one hundred years after the lifetime of the Patriarch Joseph! Well, the whole of the Theban Legion were Christians. The African branch of the Church was one of those which flourished most in the earliest ages of Christianity; and at the very beginning of the third century, (some seventy or eighty years before the time of Maximian's march into Gaul,) we read of the learned Clement of Alexandria presiding there over a regular college for training the clergy, and a few years later we have St. Cyprian of Carthage, heading, as Metropolitan, the Bishops of Mauritania and Numidia, other districts in Africa; which shows how thoroughly the True Faith had made its way all over that continent; so that it was only natural that a regiment formed there should be a Christian one; moreover, its commander, a young Roman of noble birth, called Mauritius, was himself a Christian, and may very likely have tried to avoid admitting any pagans amongst his soldiers.

" As long as this regiment was in the East with Diocletian, it seems to have been left to worship its God in its own way, and to have been distinguished only for its valour and good service; and doubtless it was in high spirits at the thought of new scenes and fresh successes that Maurice led his men from the gorgeous, imperial city of Nicomedia across the dancing waters of the Bosphorus—through the rich plains and rapid rivers between the southern mountains of Thrace, golden with cornfields and purple with vineyards—over the snowy passes of the great Mount Hæmus, further north, with its mines of precious stones and metals— and then, crossing the river Dravus, passed up through the chestnut and pine forests of Illyricum, (startling the herds of wild deer, and rousing the wild boar in his den,) and amongst the mines of quicksilver and copper, rock crystal, and marble, in its northern mountains; till they reached the Roman town of Polis, at the southern point of what we now call Capo d'Istria, where they would most likely take ship and cross the Adriatic sea to the port of Hadria, in Italy, immediately opposite. There is a geography lesson for you!"

"Shall we find all those places on the map, Uncle Max?"

"That depends on what map you look in! If you have a map of the ancient Roman Empire, you will find the names I have given you; but if you look in a modern atlas, you will have to take Turkey and Dalmatia for Thrace and Illyricum, the Balkan Mountains for Mount Hæmus, Poli for Polis, and Chioggia for Hadria.

"Well, then there would be the easier march through the level plain on the banks of the river Po to Milan, (then called Mediolanum,) the capital of the western half of the Roman Empire, where Maurice and his brother officers had to pay their respects to

the Emperor Maximian on joining his court
and army; and very likely there were great
entertainments and *fêtes* in honour of their
arrival, and perhaps the Legion was reviewed
by the emperor. Then Maximian assembled
his whole army, and set out on his march
into Gaul.

" A gallant sight it must have been to
watch the crested helmets and prancing
horses gleaming amongst the chestnut woods
and vine trellises near Aosta, and then
winding their way up through the mountains
to the steep passes of the Pennine Alps.
This was in those days the best known of
the Alpine passes, and there are some steps
cut in the rock, still to be seen near the
great Hospice on Mount St. Bernard, of
which you have often heard, that belonged
to a temple built by the Romans to their
god, Jupiter Penninus."

" Oh, Uncle Max, is that the Mount St.
Bernard where the dogs find people in the
snow, and fetch somebody to help them?"

"Yes, Mab—the Hospice, or House of Refuge, there, was founded in the tenth century, by a good man, called Bernard of Menthon; but before that there had been a chapel, and some rough shelter for benighted travellers, for about a hundred years. The good Augustinian monks who live there now, give up their lives to rescuing and helping travellers in the snowy season, which lasts for nine months of the year— and are always ready to give food, and bed, and kindness, to any one who asks their hospitality. They are good botanists, and their observations of all sorts of curious facts in natural history, whether of plants or animals or the weather, have been very useful to scientific men, who make such things their study.

"But when Maximian and his army crossed the St. Bernard by the rugged, winding road that had been used ever since a Roman colony had been settled at Colonia Augusta, (now called Aosta,) twenty-six years B. C., the temple of Jupiter Penninus stood there in all its pride, and St. Maurice and his soldiers little thought, as they passed it in grief and indignation, that, long after, the ground where it had stood would be sanctified by the noble charities of their fellow-servants of the true God!

"Which of our Lord's parables do these monks make you think of?" added Uncle Max, turning suddenly upon Hugh, who started and hesitated at being thus roused from his dreamy enjoyment of the story.

"I don't know," he said; "I wasn't thinking of any at all!"

"Well, wake up, and use your own mind, then!" said his uncle. "I can't lend you mine for nothing like this! I want it myself."

Thus urged, Hugh knit his brows, and considered; and Mabel pursed up her mouth, and looked as if occupied in most important thoughts.

"I can't tell—I can't remember which it

is," said she, presently; "but there's something about 'I was a stranger, and ye took me in.'"

"Oh, 'the sheep and the goats!'" exclaimed Hugh. "'Inasmuch as ye have done it unto one of the least of these My brethren, ye have done it unto Me [1]!' Isn't that it, Uncle Max?"

"Yes, that is what I wanted; and for the sake of some day hearing those words these monks are willing even to 'lay down their lives for the brethren!' *I* call them as 'good soldiers of Jesus Christ' as St. Maurice and his Legion, though they wear black cassocks instead of glittering armour, and their names are not handed down to us as Saints and Martyrs! Eh, Hugh?"

"I haven't heard all about St. Maurice and his Legion yet!" said Hugh, rather grandly, "so I can't judge."

"You young wiseacre! who asked you to

[1] St. Matt. xxv. 40.

judge? I may have my own opinion, I suppose! But people always think more of dead heroes than living ones!" added Uncle Max. " You missed a fine opportunity of making a sensation by not being killed in that grand tumble of yours, Hugh!"

" Oh, Uncle Max ! " exclaimed Mabel, reproachfully; while Hugh coloured furiously, and bit his lips as if that fall was a sore subject.

" Well, lad," said Uncle Max, laying a kind hand on his shoulder, " are you thinking me very unfeeling ? I don't think 1 am"— and the quick, tight clasp, in which Hugh's hand seized his, showed that he did not think so either; " only you know we agreed that I was to remind you sometimes of that warning against bumptiousness ! and I have been fancying you were rather high and mighty to-day ! "

" I'm sure, Uncle Max," said Mabel, half-crying, " Hugh hasn't been boasting at all lately about his climbing or anything else !

And you know he *can* climb better than anybody else—and—"

" Hush, Mab!" interrupted Hugh, hastily.

And Uncle Max laughed, and said, as he kissed her, " You are a loyal little sister, Puss, and I am a crabbed old uncle, am I not? I must try and make amends by going on with my story."

" Yes," said Mabel, gravely—" and, please, don't talk so much in the middle—it interrupts so ! "

And as soon as he and Hugh could recover from their laughter at this speech, Uncle Max went on.

" Well, the pass was safely crossed, and then the army had to descend through the pine forests on the other side, passing the great waterfall formed by the river Dranse, and the deep gully where the river is joined by a foaming torrent from one of the higher glaciers, and the ancient Roman milestone which is still to be seen in the little village of St. Pierre ; and then over more gentle slopes, with the great mountains rising on all sides, and the river winding through the midst, to the beautiful valley of the Rhone, where they received orders to encamp near the town of Octodurus, (now called Martigny,) and rest, after their long mountain march.

" It was near sunset, on a beautiful day in September, that Maurice, having seen his men comfortably quartered, and given his last orders for the night, reined in his horse, as he was riding slowly back to his own tent, and exclaimed, pointing to a rocky hill overlooking the town,

" ' How say you, Candidus, shall we climb yonder hill, and see the sun go down behind these icy spear-points that bristle so fiercely against the sky ? '

" ' In good faith,' replied the grey-haired veteran to whom he spoke, ' I have had enough of climbing to suffice me for many a day ! But here is Exuperius railing at the damp and heat of this valley, and full of mad schemes for reaching those same white peaks. I doubt not he will readily be your companion, and I will abide here with the men while you play your pranks!'

"'Well for us that we have one older and wiser than ourselves to stand us in such good stead!' laughed Maurice. 'You have saved us from many a heedless scrape ere now, old comrade!'

"'And shall doubtless be required to do so again!' remarked Candidus, dryly. 'Farewell to sense and discretion when you two are off duty together! You are well enough by yourself, Primicerius; but that madcap is enough to make a fool of King Solomon!'

"'King Solomon made a fool of himself!' retorted the gay young officer who rode on Maurice's right. 'Talk not treason against your superior officers, O Candidus!'

"'Talk not you so lightly, O Exuperius!' said Maurice, gravely—'I will have no joking words concerning aught mentioned in Holy Writ. You know my rule. But, come, since

our good friend here is willing to keep guard
in our absence, let us play our pranks while
we may! We know not how soon the
Bagaudæ may end them for us.'

" And throwing their reins to the armour-
bearers, who at their commanders' signal
came running up, the two young nobles
sprang from their horses, and struck out of
the beaten path and up the hill-side.

" 'A steep climb that!' exclaimed Exuperius, as, on reaching the top, he flung himself on the grass to rest; 'but, in good truth,
this is worth the trouble!'

" And Maurice's face said the same, as he
stood with folded arms looking away over
the beautiful scene spread out before them.

" On one side lay the valley of the Rhone,
parts of it still bright with the evening sun-
beams, in which the winding river glittered
like a silver thread between its green banks.
On the other, the great snowy mountains
rose range above range — the lower ones
in purple shadow, the higher glowing with

every shade of gold and orange, pink and crimson—while, shut in by these giants, and clustering all about the foot of the hills, on one of which the two friends now stood, were the white tents of Maximian's camp, where the crested helmets and glittering shields of the soldiers went gleaming to and fro; and the busy hum of voices and shrill notes of the trumpet rose up full of life. and bustle, as the men prepared their evening meal, or tethered their horses, or burnished their armour, before turning in for the night.

" ' The Augustus has found a fair nest to rest in!' said Exuperius, after a while. 'Yet I would as soon our men were quartered higher up—the heat and damp of that valley may breed some fever amongst them. How say you, shall we move on to-morrow, and seek fresher breezes?'

" ' Not unless it seems really necessary,' replied Maurice, sitting down by him. 'I would not willingly annoy the Augustus—

and he may well think the place which he
chooses for his own men good enough for
ours.'

" ' He has seemed well pleased with our
doings hitherto. We could not have had a
better reception than he gave us at Mediolanum! And he could not complain of care
for our troops. They say you are already high
in his favour, Mauritius, as you were in that
of our most gracious Prince Diocletianus.

" ' And they who say so are already jealous
of us, and will spare no pains to make us
odious in the emperor's eyes! "Put not
your trust in princes," Exuperius, "nor in
any child of man, for there is no help in
them!" "It is better to trust in the Lord
than to put any confidence in man." '

" ' Granted, my friend,' responded Exuperius, brightly. ' But why so solemn and full
of foreboding? You are not wont to meet
troubles half way; and to trust in the Lord
is to be kept in perfect peace!'

" ' You are right,' said Maurice, quickly;

'and it is not that I fear what man can do unto us, but I fear what we may do unto ourselves! I have heard rumours,' he added, in a lower tone, 'of a great sacrifice to the gods of Rome to be commanded throughout the army, and what if our men should be led away to join in this service of devils, and deny the Lord of Glory?'

"'They could not be so base!' cried Exuperius. 'If they were, I would strike the traitors dead where they stood!'

"'And if they remained steadfast in the faith the pagans would save you that trouble; so either way the poor fellows seem likely to be in evil case!' replied his friend, smiling. 'And, after all, it may be but rumour, and there may be no such fiery trial in store for them. But let us pray more earnestly for them that their faith fail not whatever happens; for it is well known that the Emperor Maximianus hath less love to his Christian subjects than his colleague Diocletianus.'

"There was silence after that for a while. Exuperius bowed his face on his hands with a shudder, all his gaiety gone for the time; and Maurice gazed across at the mountains and the sunset, as if he saw beyond them.

"The sun was sinking fast now, and only the highest peaks still reflected its bright colouring. As its lower edge dipped behind the snowy points, Maurice touched his companion's arm, and, laying their helmets on the ground, the two rose to their feet, and began in clear and mellow tones to sing the Latin hymn used by the Christians in their daily Vesper Office, or Evensong, as we call it now: ' *Te lucis ante terminum.*'"

"What does that mean, Uncle Max?"

"Can *you* tell us, Hugh?" said Uncle Max, turning to the boy.

"' *Te,*' Thee—' *ante terminum,*' before the ending—' *lucis,*' of the light. Isn't that it?"

"Yes. Now here is a translation of the whole hymn, if you care to see it."

And Uncle Max drew from his pocket a

little book of Prayers which he opened and handed to Mabel, who read aloud the following hymn :—

"'Now that the daylight dies away,
  Ere we lie down and sleep,
Thee, Maker of the world, we pray,
  To own us, and to keep.

"'Let dreams depart, and visions fly,
  The offspring of the night ;
Keep us, as shrines, beneath Thine Eye,
  Pure in our foes' despite.

"'This grace on Thy redeemed confer,
  Father, co-equal Son,
And Holy Ghost, the Comforter ;
  Eternal Three in One.   Amen.'"

"Is that really the very hymn Maurice and Ex— Ex— I can't say the other name, Uncle Max."

"Exuperius," said Hugh, with a superior air.

"Yes—that's it. Well, I mean is that the very same hymn they sang?"

"Most likely, Mab—I believe it is one of the very old Latin hymns."

"How nice it must have sounded up there

amongst the mountains!" remarked Hugh, thoughtfully. "Would there be an echo, Uncle Max?"

"A good many, I should think. Probably the sound would be given back by heights which had never before rung with the praises of the true God! They little knew how soon they were to *see* Him praised!" replied Uncle Max, his face lighting up with enthusiasm. Then, after a minute or two, he went on.

"When they had finished the hymn, Maurice stood for a few moments with bent head and clasped hands, and then turned as if to descend the hill; but his friend stopped him.

"'Can we not say Vespers here?' he said. 'This is a fitter oratory than yonder noisy camp!'

"'It were not wise for the Commander of a Legion to be benighted afar from his men,' replied Maurice, 'and the shadows are gathering fast around us. Moreover, methinks there is some stir in the camp. Turn your sharp eyes upon our Legion, Exuperius; what seems it to you is going on amongst them?'

" Exuperius swung round on his heel, and scanned the camp spread out at their feet, as keenly as the growing twilight would allow.

" 'What means this?' he exclaimed, hastily. 'The fellows are striking their tents! It cannot be mutiny! Yet I can believe any evil from contact with those heathen dogs!'

" And as he muttered the last words through his set teeth, he turned to spring down the steep path, his sword already half-drawn. Mauritius was before him, moving with a light, steady step, that gained ground as rapidly as his friend's more daring leaps, which occasionally resulted in a stumble amongst the rocky fragments with which the hill-side was strewn.

" It was not long before they reached the

outskirts of the camp, and made their way
to the quarter which Maurice had selected
for his Theban Legion. Here all was bustle
and scurry; men hurrying hither and thither
—some unfastening the tent-pins, others
untethering the horses, others hastily assum-
ing the armour they had not long before laid
aside for the night. Catching the rein of a
horse, which had just been saddled, from the
man who held it, Maurice sprang upon its
back, and, standing up in the stirrups,
shouted in the ringing, trumpet-like tones
his men knew so well:

" ' What means this turmoil? Men, to
your tents, till I know the reason of this!'

" There was an instant lull, and the men
fell into order at the tent-doors—while one
of the lower centurions came forward and
said, respectfully,

" ' His Excellency Candidus, First Centurion of the Second Cohort, hath issued an
order that the Legion should withdraw to a
distance from the rest of the camp!'

"'In good truth he has!' exclaimed
Exuperius, impatiently. 'And for what
cause, I pray you?'

"'Peace, Exuperius!' said Maurice, the
easy frankness of the past hour replaced by
all the dignity of the commanding officer.
'Suffer *me* to speak! Where is the Centurion Candidus?' he added, turning to the
junior officer who had spoken.

'He made as though he would go to your
Excellency's tent!' was the reply.

"Without more ado, Maurice put spurs
to the horse he had mounted, and dashed
towards the rising ground where his own
tent towered above the rest; while the fleet
Exuperius darted after him on foot, till,
passing a horse, which one of the soldiers
had just untethered, he snatched the halter
from the man's hand, sprang upon its back
at one bound, and sped after his leader
without saddle or bridle, as he had often
raced with his companions through the
Campagna near his Roman home.

" It was not many minutes before they reined up at the door of the commander's tent, where Candidus stood with folded arms, looking worn and anxious.

" ' Thank God you are come!' he exclaimed, coming forward to salute Maurice respectfully, as he threw himself from the saddle, saying to the men-at-arms who came forward to take charge of the horses, ' Take these back to their owners, and bring out my black charger: not Lucia, she has been on service all day.'

" ' Auster is already saddled, my lord!' replied one of the men; and, stooping his lofty head, Maurice passed on into the tent, followed by Candidus and Exuperius.

" ' Well?' he said, facing round upon the elder, when the curtain had fallen behind them.

" ' The decree is gone forth,' replied the veteran, gravely. ' There is a sacrifice to the gods to-morrow at dawn!'

" ' A sacrifice to devils!' burst forth

Exuperius, hotly. 'But we are exempt, Candidus? We were ever exempted from such abominations by the Eastern Augustus!'

" ' *None* are exempt,' was the grave response. 'We serve the Western Augustus now, young man!'

" ' Suffer me to go and beard the emperor in his tent, now, before he sleeps?' exclaimed the young man, turning to Maurice. ' It is monstrous; it will cause sedition; the Legion will rebel as one man. We shall have civil war in the camp!'

" ' Never, while I am in command!' said Maurice, resolutely. 'We may have martyrdoms—I think we shall; but not brawls and tumults, so help me God! What command have you given, Candidus?'

" ' To withdraw to a rising ground three leagues off. I called a council of the junior officers, and we agreed that you would have the men removed from all intercourse with the idolaters; and there being little daylight left, I gave the order without awaiting your return.'

" ' Then it must be executed forthwith,' said the young commander. 'Otherwise I should have chosen rather to take the first flush of dawn than the last rays of twilight for even so short a move in a strange land! But some explanation must be sent to the Augustus — otherwise he might be justly wroth. No, not you, Exuperius—I cannot trust your hot head in the royal presence just now!' he added, smiling, as the younger officer was about to speak. ' Go you to the front; urge the men to all speed in preparing for the march; and yourself go forward with a reconnoitering party to see what difficulties lie in the way, and take up the ground for the rest. Candidus, you must be my envoy to Maximianus.'

" 'You will tell him the truth?' exclaimed Exuperius. 'You will say that we cannot deny our Lord?'

" ' It may yet not be required of us—no

need to *provoke* persecution!' said his calmer friend. Adding, with some sternness, as the young man made a gesture of impatience, 'the despatches are *my* affairs. Go you to your post!'

"''Tis well thy heart is better than thy head, young man!' remarked Candidus, bluntly, as Exuperius bowed and withdrew without another word; for gentle as Maurice was, no one dared to dispute his commands when given in that tone.

"It was not many minutes before Candidus was despatched on his errand, and then Maurice lifted the curtain that shut off part of his tent, and throwing himself on his knees beside his rough soldier's bed, poured forth the tumult of anxious thoughts, the weary weight of care, the wild excitement of mingled aspiration and dread, so resolutely hidden under his calm, thoughtful manner; and only told to the One Friend Who could fully understand, the One Leader Who could unerringly direct him.

"A few minutes later he was again at his tent door, where his black charger was pawing the ground, while his suite of attendant officers, already mounted, waited like statues, for his word of command.

"'Has the First Centurion Exuperius marched with the vanguard?' asked Maurice, as he sprang into his saddle, and turned his horse's head in the direction where a mass of figures, scarcely seen in the gathering darkness, was moving quickly but silently away from the camp.

"'He has, my lord!' replied one of the staff, respectfully riding up to his side, while the whole group clattered in behind them, their crested helmets flashing back the pale rays of the harvest moon which was just rising above the mountains.

"'It is well,' said the young commander. 'We shall lead the main column—the Centurion Candidus commands the rear.'"

"It was midnight before the last tent was pitched near the little village of Agaunum, (now St. Maurice;) and long after the soldiers were fast asleep there were anxious faces and eager voices in their Commander's tent.

" Candidus had come thither to report his visit to the Emperor, and Maurice had desired the other officers to be present. They came trooping in—sunburnt veterans with many a scar, young men eager for some glorious dints in their bran-new armour— till the tent was quite full. And then Candidus told how he had failed to reach the Emperor's presence; how his message had been sullenly received by the Tribune or General Officer to whom he had delivered it; how great preparations were being made for the idolatrous festivities next day; and the drunken mirth already begun boded ill for those who would not join in it. And then there was a pause, and an angry mur-mur ran through the assembly. It ceased as Maurice, who was seated at the table, rose to his full height and looked gravely round.

"'My brothers,' he said, and his low clear tones rang through the tent, 'I like not that sound. Have patience with me a moment, and let us face this matter calmly, as we have faced many a death struggle together!'

"'Meseems we have a death struggle before us now that will be fiercer than all, and give us little glory!' said a young officer who stood near him.

"'That it will be our fiercest I well believe!' said Maurice, calmly, turning towards him. 'That it will be our most glorious, I heartily hope. How think you, Procopius? Is it more honourable to take life or to lose it? To fight for an earthly Prince, or to suffer for a heavenly?'

"There was a silence—the fierce eyes of the soldier fell before the grave searching glance of his commander; and presently Maurice went on, turning again to the whole assembly.

"'My friends, you know well that I never hide from you whatever danger lies before us—that I never deceive you with fair words—and therefore have I summoned you hither this night, that we may speak together openly of the morrow's temptation. You all know that we shall be bidden to these great Games, in which it is not lawful for Christians to take part. You know the fearful abyss of sin to which they too often lead, besides giving homage to gods many and lords many. But to us there is but One God, the Father, by Whom are all things, and we in Him; and One Lord Jesus Christ, by Whom are all things, and we by Him!' Every head was bowed reverently at the Holy Name, and a low 'Amen!' burst from every mouth.

"He paused for a moment, glancing from face to face, as though to read whether that 'Amen' did indeed come from the heart—then he went on:

"'My friends, it is no easy battle that is before us! We shall be called disloyal, traitors and cowards. We may be scourged, decimated[1], slaughtered — cruelly tortured, even as were our holy Fathers the Apostles and the blessed Martyrs, who have borne witness among all nations for the True God. Can you bear this? Can you meet death calmly in the camp and unarmed, as you would—as many of you *have* done, in the hottest battlefields? Or will you deny the Lord of Glory, and put Him to an open shame, that you may enjoy the pleasures of sin for a season? Choose you this day Whom you will serve! Choose you which you will wear! The sword and laurel-wreath of earth, or the palm and golden crown of Heaven?'

"And, as he ended, he suddenly drew his sword from its jewelled scabbard and pointed it upwards. Then there was a clash of weapons, for the warriors around him with one consent unsheathed their swords also, and, lifting them as he had done, exclaimed,

---

[1] See p. 67 for explanation of this word.

"'The Lord He is God! We are His servants. We will do whatsoever pleaseth Him!'

"'Then,' said Maurice, 'let us bow our knees to the God and Father of our Lord Jesus Christ, that He may with the temptation make us a way to escape, that we may be able to bear it.'

"And the clang of armour again rang through the tent as the warriors knelt, while their chief, in a few fervent words, asked for strength and patience for themselves and their men in the trial which awaited them; and then, when all had joined in the Lord's Prayer, they went silently out, till Maurice was left once more alone.

"Not for long, however. As he sat on his bed with his face buried in his hands after all were gone he heard the sentry outside his tent give the challenge, and the next moment Exuperius stood in the doorway.

E

"'Is aught amiss?' asked Maurice, starting up.

"'No,' answered the young man; 'but I could not sleep, and I did not suppose you could, so I thought I might come and sit here a while.'

"He looked pale and haggard as he came forward into the light of the oil-lamp that stood on the table, and Maurice held out his hand, saying warmly,

"Welcome as ever, my brother! Come, sit here, and let us talk together.'

"'Truly I need thy brave words, Mauritius! for I am turning craven, I believe. Never before have I known fear; but to-night I am a perfect fool, and dread my own shadow!'

"He spoke fiercely, as if enraged at his own weakness. And Maurice answered him calmly and gently, as if such a confession were the most natural thing in the world.

"You are weary, and have fasted long, and that makes cowards of the bravest men.

The morning will chase away these fancies, and you will marvel if you indeed had them. But I myself have some fear——'

"'You!' cried Exuperius. 'Why, I hardly hoped to find myself in such good company!'

"'I fear not keeping my hand off my sword, if the pagans draw theirs upon us!' replied his friend. 'I fear being unable to show my men the truer glory of dying as a Christian, rather than as a soldier!'

"Exuperius caught his hand.

"'That is my dread!' he said, hastily. 'I cannot face the thought of being hanged like a dog, or crucified like a traitor! Generation after generation of our family have fallen gloriously fighting for their country, or lived to return as conquerors to the gates of Rome, there to be welcomed with songs and dances, and crowned with laurel at the Capitol—and I thought——'

"'You thought to have laid a dinted shield and a laurel crown at the feet of my fair sister—is it not so?' said Maurice, as the young man hesitated. 'But, trust me, my friend, Lucia would esteem it higher honour to have been the chosen bride of one who willingly gave up earthly fame to bear witness for the truth! Does not her eye ever kindle at mention of the noble name of Stephen the Deacon, the first among those who have joyfully sealed with their blood that confession of our common Faith which we as yet have but made with our lips? We have glorious leaders to cheer us on, Exuperius! "men who have hazarded their lives for the Name of the Lord Jesus!" men who "loved not their lives unto the death." Let us not, in the thought that we are soldiers of Rome, forget that we were first "soldiers of Christ," and therefore pledged to "endure hardness" for Him, though it be to death—so saith the holy Paul in that letter unto the Bishop of Ephesus which he wrote in our city while awaiting the sentence of the tyrant Nero.'

" 'You speak bravely, Mauritius, as you ever do—as you did long ago in the days when I could only answer, " Almost thou persuadest me to be a Christian !" said Exuperius, sadly. Then, with a sudden flash of his old merriment, he added, ' And I fear me you had waited long for another answer, O Friend, had not the Donna Lucia taken me in the rear, when I deemed I had repulsed *your* attack for the time!'

" Maurice started up, and grasped his friend's arm. ' Exuperius,' he said, sternly, ' is *that* your reason for professing this most holy faith? Is it only to win favour with *her* that you bear the seal of Baptism? If so, I marvel not that you quail at the thought of martyrdom.'

" Exuperius flung off his hand, and rising, strode to the tent-door; but the next moment he swung round, and came back to his friend's side.

" ' You are hard on me,' he said, half fiercely. ' A while ago I should not have

borne patiently anything so like an insult ;
but there is some truth in your words, and
therefore I will answer you.   It *was* for her
sake ; it is not *now*.'

" ' Pardon me, my friend ! ' said Maurice ;
' but it was a terrible dread, and I longed to
have it laid by your own truth-speaking lips.
Nay, brother, give me your hand ; let us not
weaken each other's heart by mistrust and
wrath, on this night, when, God knows ! we
need courage and cheering as we never
needed it yet ! '   His tone grew weary, and
Exuperius, glancing at his worn, anxious
face, was softened at once.

" ' Why do I chafe and weary you with
my folly ? ' he exclaimed.   ' Forget all this,
Mauritius, and lie down and rest.   I will
abide, and watch beside you till the dawn.'

" ' Nay,' said his friend, smiling ; ' with
God above, and my Legion around me, what
need have I of watchers ?   We will both
slumber, my friend.   He will give His
angels charge over us.   May St. Raphael

spread his wings above our heads, and St. Michael's sword keep guard beside our door ! '

" 'Ay, and St. Gabriel rouse us for the conflict at break of day ; for, by God's grace, you shall see me play my part as no luke-warm Christian to - morrow ! ' exclaimed Exuperius, throwing back his head proudly.

" Maurice looked at him a little anxiously ; but he did not speak, only in a minute he said, ' Let us commend ourselves to the most High God !' and soon the tired soldier had fallen asleep.

" The next morning dawned brightly upon the Alpine valley, and found the Theban Legion drawn up in close square round the knoll on which stood their commander's tent, to begin their day by worshipping together their One God ; while from the rest of the camp came sounds of busy preparation and noisy mirth, which told that the Games would soon begin.

" The Matin, or morning hymn, sung

by the Christians, had scarcely died away amongst the mountain echoes, when a messenger arrived in hot haste from the Emperor's quarters, and demanded an audience of Maurice.

" He was led through the lines to the open space in front of the commander's tent, where Maurice and his staff courteously received him.

" ' Primicerius of the Legion of the Thebaid!' he said, haughtily, ' it is matter of surprise and displeasure to our most noble Augustus that you have not yet caused preparation to be made in your camp to assist in the solemn sacrifice to the great gods of Rome, ordained to take place this day. It is the command of our august Master that such preparation be made by you without delay ; and that you, with the principal officers of your suite, present yourselves immediately in the Imperial camp, in order to take part in the noble games there to be forthwith held ! '

" There was a low murmur of dissatisfaction amongst the officers, and Exuperius' hand was on his sword; but Maurice looked round reprovingly, and there was silence again, as he ànswered gravely but courteously,

" 'That you should be the bearer of such orders is to me cause of great regret; since, for the first time in my career as a soldier of Rome, it is my grievous task to decline obeying her behests. Say to the Augustus, that we are ready to a man to lay down our lives in his service, but we cannot worship his gods, since we serve the Lord Christ.'

" ' Is *this* your answer to the most noble Emperor? Think well, O Primicerius, before you repeat such insolence !'

" 'We have already thought,' said Maurice, calmly; ' and there is nothing to reconsider. One of my officers shall accompany you on your return to the Imperial camp, to set forth before the Augustus our eager and entire submission to all other his commands; but our necessity in this one thing to hold us aloof. With his gracious permission, we will abide quietly in our tents until the games shall be ended, when we shall be the more refreshed and strengthened to do battle with the enemies of Rome.'

" 'Madman!' said the envoy, contemptuously. 'Think you to move the Augustus from his purpose by such idle tattle? Think you that he will now show special favour to you Christians, when it is to the destruction of the Christians throughout Gaul that he now leads us? Movers of sedition that you ever are!'

"An ominous murmur ran throughout the camp; and even Maurice's eyes flashed; and he opened his lips for some indignant answer; but it did not come, and an expression of bitter pain passed over his face as he looked along the gallant ranks of his Legion before he answered calmly,

" 'Methinks these rash words formed no

part of your message; in which case it were better breeding and wiser judgment to refrain from insulting us in our own camp. You have our answer to the most noble Augustus—there needs no further parley.'

" ' You speak too fast,' returned the envoy, enraged at his self-possession. ' I have somewhat more to say. The commands of that mighty Emperor, whom you so audaciously set at nought, enjoin, that should you and your Legion dare impiously to deny the great gods of Rome, and treasonably to resist the Imperial mandate, the Legion shall forthwith be decimated!'

" There was a dead silence for a moment —a sort of breathless pause at this declaration of open warfare on the part of the Emperor; and the look of pain returned to Maurice's face as he said,

" ' These tidings are no surprise to me. Had it been otherwise, you had not dared to speak to us as you have done. My men shall answer you now.'

" Then he raised his voice, moving forward a step or two, so as to be seen and heard by the more distant ranks, and said,

" ' My Brothers! there lie before us this day two things—the praise of men and the praise of our Lord Christ. The Augustus says to us, " Look round upon the good things of this world ; see the spoils, the glory, the rank—all these things will I give ye, if ye will fall down and worship my gods!" And He, the King Eternal, Invisible, *He* says to us, " Be ye faithful unto death, and I will give ye a Crown of Life !" My Brothers, which shall we choose ?'

" And then from the whole of that glittering throng of armed warriors there arose a shout, 'The Lord! the Lord Christ! We are His servants!'

" ' Are ye then content to die for Him in camp, as ye would have died for Rome in battle ?'

" And the answer came surging up the

lines—'We will lay down our lives for His sake!'

"'So help us God!' said the Commander, solemnly. Then, turning to the envoy, who stood by astonished and awed, he said, with a smile, 'There is no use in pressing us further; we are ready to suffer whatever it may please the Emperor to lay upon us; though, were I worthy to advise, I would suggest that his foes be overcome ere his Legions be crippled; but we cannot be untrue to our First Master; and He says to us, "Thou shalt have no other gods but Me."'

"The officer bowed silently and prepared to go; and Maurice beckoned Candidus to his side, and desired him to proceed also to the Imperial tent and plead their cause with the Emperor himself.

"'I will say what I can, Primicerius,' said the old soldier; 'but I much fear 'twill be in vain.'

"'That is as God wills!' replied Maurice.

'Your thought is mine, O Candidus; but I may not lose the lives of my men for lack of straining every nerve to save them; neither may we court that martyrdom which, if assigned to us unsought, will be our highest honour.   You have a wise head and a discreet tongue, wherefore do your best for our valiant Legion.   And we will give ourselves unto prayer.'

"Candidus rode away; and Maurice, turning back from watching him start, found Exuperius' eyes fixed imploringly upon him.   He knew what it had cost the eager youth not to beg for the post of envoy, and smiled affectionately at him as he said, 'Go with him, Exuperius; but remember, you are under his authority.'   And with a respectful salute, and sign of assent, Exuperius darted after the old soldier; and Maurice, on his great black charger, paced slowly through his camp, speaking words of sympathy and encouragement to all, and pausing at each division to offer a short prayer that his men might be true to the watchword he had given them—'Faithful unto death.'

"Each rank as he passed on obeyed his directions to await the Imperial decree in silent prayer, and knelt down quietly in their places; so that when the ambassadors returned from the Imperial camp, surrounded by a strong escort of royal troops, it was to see the whole of the Legion kneeling, grave and motionless as the great mountains which encompassed them, save for the lips which moved in prayer, and their Commander sitting statue-like on his noble warhorse at the door of his tent awaiting their approach.

"The scoffs and laughter which burst forth from the heathen soldiery when first they entered the Christian camp gradually died away as they passed through line after line of silent kneeling warriors, and a superstitious fear fell on them which changed their mockery into hatred; and they were

scowling faces upon which Maurice's eye
rested as the band halted at the foot of the
knoll on which his tent stood, and suffered
Candidus and Exuperius to ride on alone to
deliver their report.

"Gravely returning their salute, Maurice
motioned them aside while he rode forward
and gave the word of command to his men,
then, when the echoing clash and clang of
arms with which the Legion rose and fell
into line had died away amongst the hills, he
turned towards them again, asking simply,
'How have ye sped?'

"'Ill, my lord!' answered Candidus, sadly.
'The Augustus would scarce hearken to our
words—and his minions insulted us sore.
But for this brave lad your message had
gone unheard; but his bold bearing and
ready wit stood us in good stead, and turned
the laugh against some of them who with-
stood us.   Methinks the Emperor coveted so
gallant a follower, and thought by patience
and flattery to win him to his side!'

"Maurice turned with his bright smile to Exuperius, who, flushing with pleasure at the unexpected praise, had kept silence till his elder had spoken, though his bright restless eyes showed how hard it was to him to do so.

"'What spake you to the Augustus, my brother?' asked Maurice.

"'I scarce know,' replied Exuperius. 'I asked him, When had a true son of Rome broken his plighted word? I said we had pledged ourselves twice—first to worship the God of heaven and earth, and, secondly, to serve Rome; and asked him how, if we broke our first vow, he could trust us to be faithful to our second? I bade him call to mind the martial games at Mediolanum whereat he so highly applauded us; and asked, were it not a pity to cut down with his own hand the veterans of whom he then said they would do him such good service? I asked him, whether were the better preparation for a great campaign—the revelry

F

with which his troops would celebrate this
sacrifice, or the solemn offices and tempe-
rate repose with which our Christian Legion
looked forth to death or victory?'

"'And what answer did he make?'

"'He said I spoke well in an evil cause,
and he would fain win me to a better
mind! And I told him he brought to my
mind a passage in our Sacred Writings,
which told how the holy Apostle Paul stood
before the noble Festus, when *he* ruled
Judea in the name of Rome, and before
King Agrippa and his fair queen, and spake
to them as never man spake to them before,
of justice, temperance, and judgment to
come; and as he looked on them in their
pomp and majesty and paganism, pitied
them from his heart, and uplifted his thin
scarred hands heavy with their clanking
chains, and cried aloud, "I would that all
that hear me were not almost, but altogether
such as I am;" and that I would say the
same to *him!*'

" ' And what said he then ? '

" ' First he called me a hare-brained fool; and then he laughed, and said I was a brave boy, and bade me abide with him while my companion took back his answer to you; but I told him I should be no true Roman if I broke faith with my commanding officer, and no true Christian if I rested in ease and safety while my brethren in the faith were persecuted or slain for the testimony of Jesus; and that my post was at the head of my cohort—to live or die!'

" God be thanked!' said Maurice, softly. 'Yet, if it be His will, I would that you might live to testify of Him by word and deed, whether in camp or in our beloved Rome!'

" ' Do not wish it!' exclaimed Exuperius, vehemently. 'Wish rather that in this massacre I may be cut down, so I may be found faithful unto death! Oh, Mauritius, I tremble lest I endure not in patience!'

" ' How spake the Blessed One to His

holy Apostle Peter?' said Maurice. "Satan hath desired to have you, that he may sift you as wheat; but I have prayed for thee, that thy faith fail not[1]." Shall not His prayers avail also for us, Exuperius? Think not of yourself, but of your men, my brother, who look to you for their example. In strengthening them, you will yourself be strengthened. But, see, yonder band of pagans grow impatient to begin their bloody work. Alas! poor souls, that know not the truth!

" ' Take up your positions, my brothers; and if we speak not again here face to face, the Lord grant us to await Him side by side in Paradise.'

" Candidus and Exuperius saluted, and rode away, to take their places at the head of the first and second cohorts; and, after despatching some other members of his staff to bear the Emperor's answer to the rest of the Legion, Maurice advanced to the centu-

[1] St. Luke xxii. 31, 32.

rion in command of the Imperial troops,
and said courteously,

" 'We will not delay you longer in the
execution of your duty.' "

" And then, Uncle Max ? " exclaimed the
children, as their uncle paused—

" Then the decimation began. You
know ——."

" But, Uncle Max, I don't understand
what that means," said Mabel.

" Suppose we make Hugh tell us, little
one. Can you, Hugh ? "

" It meant putting every tenth man to
death, didn't it ? " said Hugh.

" In this instance it did, certainly; but
the punishment was not always death. It
meant, I think, the selection by lot of every
tenth man for punishment, more or less
severe, according to the offence committed;
and was inflicted when too large a number
had been drawn into mutiny to admit of
individual punishment."

" And was a tenth of the Legion killed

for being Christians?" asked Hugh, indignantly.

"Yes," answered his uncle; "and not only a tenth, but a fifth, Hugh; for the soldiers remaining firm in their refusal to take part in the heathen sacrifices after the first decimation, another was commanded, Maximian being by this time furious at the failure of his efforts to bend them to his will; and his soldiers, excited and rendered bloodthirsty by witnessing the first execution."

"What a fool that man must have been!" broke out Hugh, "not to see that he was helping his enemies by cutting down his finest troops!"

"Ah, Hugh, a man is sure to make a fool of himself if he lets himself become the slave of his passions, instead of their master! Maximian was a brave soldier and a wise general; but he had never learnt that 'greater is he that ruleth his spirit, than he that taketh a city;' and so he had never tried to get rid of the coarseness that made him cruel, and the self-love that made him tyrannical! Consequently his evil passions grew bigger and bigger, and warped his judgment, and led him into all sorts of blunders; but then, remember, he was a pagan, and had not 'the power of the Father to protect him, and the wisdom of the Son to enlighten him, and the peace of the Holy Ghost to strengthen him, as you and I have.'"

"But, Uncle Max," interrupted Mabel, "why does God let people be killed for loving Him?"

"The old puzzle, eh, Mab? Well, don't you see, that if Maximian had been kind and indulgent, and not tried to oblige the Christian Legion to join in his heathen sacrifice, the chances are, first, one and then another of the Christian soldiers would have strayed out to look on; then, most likely, some of the weaker and less earnest among them might have been drawn into taking

some part in the drinking and idolatrous
games ; and these might have persuaded
others of their comrades to do the same ;
and if once the main body of the Legion had
become corrupted, the efforts of Maurice
and the other officers would have been power-
less to restore discipline, and lead them
back to their broken faith. You cannot tell,
little Mab, what the spiritual dangers were
that beset those poor men, and might have
destroyed both body and soul in hell ! Was
it not in mercy that their wise and loving
Master led them through this short, though
sharp, trial of faith, into His Blessed Presence, instead of suffering them to live on
in prosperity here, and perhaps to be for
ever separated from Him by the poisonous
wiles and crafts of the devil ? ”

“ Yes, I see,” said Mabel, slowly. “ It is
like what nurse said when our baby brother
died. She said we mustn't think it hard for
him to be taken away, because the angels
could take better care of him than even

papa and mamma, and Hugh and I; and that our Blessed Lord would bring him up Himself, so that he would be always good and happy."

" Nurse was quite right, my child!" said Uncle Max, kissing the little face that looked up so seriously at him; and then, turning to Hugh, who was looking out of the window with knit brows and a some-what perplexed expression, he laid his hand on his shoulder, and asked, kindly, " And what are *you* thinking of, my boy?"

" There's something in the Psalms you made me think of," said Hugh; " and I can't tell what it is! Something about ' precious balms' and ' wickedness!'"

" ' Let not their precious balms break my head; yea, I will pray yet against their wickedness.' Do you mean that?"

" Yes; isn't that the sort of thing you meant when you said it was better for the men to be shot than flattered by the pagans?"

" Lest the flattery which seemed like pre-cious balm should prove to be poison," said his uncle, with the quick comprehension of his thought that was the chief tie between them. " Yes, Hugh. I am glad you are learning to dive with your eyes open ! "

" What *do* you mean ? " exclaimed Mabel, while Hugh looked round with a little laugh, and answered before his uncle could speak, "Don't you know, Mab, those pretty shells and things I brought you when I was having swim-ming lessons last spring?　Well, I couldn't have seen to get them if I hadn't kept my eyes open when I dived ; I should only have seen things at the top of the water ; and Uncle Max means that the Bible is like the sea, full of wonderful things, only we can't find them at first till we have learnt how to look for them."

" And that takes a life-time to learn ! " said Uncle Max, gravely. " You and I are only at the beginning of our lesson yet, Hugh ; and we shall not finish it till

' through the grave, and gate of death, we pass to our joyful Resurrection;' and then ' we shall know even as we are known.' "

" I don't think *I* know how to look for them *at all*, Uncle Max!" said Mabel, rather sadly.

" The Holy Spirit will teach you, dear, in His own good time," said her uncle, very gently. " I will tell you a little prayer out of the Psalms to say in your heart whenever you are going to read the Bible, or hear it read — 'O Lord, open Thou mine eyes, that I may see the wondrous things of Thy Law.' Do you think you can remember that ? "

" Oh, yes, Uncle Max! I will always say it," whispered Mabel, softly, nestling closer within the strong arm that held her so tenderly. " And now, please, will you go on with the story ? "

And Uncle Max went on.

" After the second decimation, there was a pause. The centurion in command of the

archers who had been acting as executioners
sent to ask for another interview with Maurice, and was received by him as before at
the entrance of his tent in full view of the
lines.

" ' Primicerius,' he exclaimed, pointing to
the gaps where had lately stood some of the
finest soldiers in the Legion, ' this is sicken-
ing work!'

" ' It is, indeed!' was the sad response;
and the officer started at sight of the white,
set face, which the young commander turned
upon him.

" ' At least save the rest of your men,' he
went on, eagerly. ' The Augustus is furious,
and vows by the Temple of Nemesis that
not one shall escape if ye persist longer in
this disobedience. I entreat you to yield
this once, and when the Emperor's anger
has cooled towards you, you may win him to
more indulgence. I myself will use my best
endeavours on your behalf, if only you will
show yourself the worthy guardian of these

valiant lives, and command your men to desist from their obstinacy ere it be too late!"

"'Regulus,' said Maurice, in the clear ringing tones which reached so far, 'the God Whose I am, and Whom I serve, has made me guardian of the lives of these gallant soldiers, not for time alone, but for Eternity! I should ill fulfil my trust were I to counsel them to forego the Crown of Glory and the endless Feast which awaits them in His Palace; in order to gain the fading wreath of earthly honour, (dear as it is to a Roman warrior,) and the fickle favour of earthly rulers. The Leader Whom *we* follow changeth not, but is "the same yesterday, to-day, and for ever."'

"'This is madness!' exclaimed the officer. 'Alas! can nothing move you? Think of the Emperor's vow. I have but just received another message to urge you to obedience under pain of utter destruction; and even now the Latin Legion begins to hem you round! I entreat you to relent ere it be too late!'

"'I have already seen the Imperial Legion advancing upon us,' replied Maurice, calmly; 'but I know that I speak the will of every one of my men, when I say that we will suffer all extremities rather than deny our Lord and lift our hand against our fellow-Christians!'

"He raised his voice as he spoke, so as to be heard along the lines nearest him, and a murmur of assent rose from all sides, and swelled louder and louder, as his words were passed from mouth to mouth, till it grew to a shout.

"'We too are Christians! We believe in One God the Father and in His Son Jesus Christ Whom He hath sent. We will die for the Faith once delivered to the Saints! Speak for us, Primicerius. Say to the Augustus that we will go forth gladly against his enemies, but not against the servants of the Lord Christ.'

"'You hear,' said Maurice, turning to the centurion, with a smile as radiant as if he had been returning from victory. 'I am but the mouthpiece—the *will* is one throughout my Legion, and that is by the power of the Holy Ghost made one with the Will of our Divine Master! I thank you for your courtesy; and I would ask you once more to take our answer to the Augustus before we die. Tell him, I pray you, what you have seen and heard—and say to him, "We have seen our companions slain without lamenting them, and we rejoice at their honour. Neither this extremity to which we are reduced, nor any provocation hath tempted us to revolt. We have arms in our hands, but we do not resist, because we had rather die innocent than live by any sin.'"

"'Farewell, Primicerius!' said Regulus, sadly. 'I would that so much resolution were shown in a better cause! It is an evil day for Rome when her bravest soldiers sacrifice honour, loyalty, and life, to a mad fancy.'

"And he departed, while Maurice gave orders that the Legion should be informed by the chief centurions, of the Emperor's resolution to massacre them all if they remained steadfast in their refusal to obey his commands; and then he, and Exuperius, and Candidus rode along the lines exhorting and encouraging the men to suffer patiently, and without resistance, whatever might come upon them.

"The sentence was soon put into execution. First came an order that the officers should be assembled and put to death at once, the Emperor hoping thus to discourage the men, and even to bring them to submit when their leaders were gone. They rode up to the vacant space in front of the Commander's tent, that noble-looking band of high-born warriors—some, veterans who had grown grey in the service of Rome, some, in the prime of manly vigour, some, still youths who had started full of eager aspirations on their first campaign. There, at Maurice's

word they dismounted, and the war-horses
in their gay trappings were led away to a
little distance by the attendants—a pro-
ceeding which Auster did not approve of,
and, with a toss of his black head swinging
the rein out of the armour-bearer's hand, he
trotted back to his master's side, and thrust
his nose into his hand. Then for the first
time Maurice's composure faltered, and
throwing his arm over his charger's neck he
half hid his face in his long black mane.

"His enemies were not slow to make
another effort to shake his firmness!

"'See,' exclaimed Regulus, who was standing by, 'even the horse would win you to
a better mind! Let not another master
ride him to victory because his own hath
died a traitor's death!'

"Exuperius sprang between them. 'You
lie!' he burst forth.

"But Maurice raised his head, and put
him gently aside.

"'He who is true to his God cannot be

G

false to his country!' he said. 'Farewell,
Auster! I would you might share my grave,
for you will grieve for me, I know; but He
Who careth for the sparrows, will surely
give you to a noble master. Now go!' He
kissed the great black forehead and put the
rein again into his armour-bearer's hand, and
Auster paced slowly and dejectedly away.

"'I have one boon to crave,' said Maurice,
turning his white resolute face upon the
officer again. 'Suffer me to live until all
my comrades are slain, that while they
need me, I may strengthen their hearts.'

"'Nay, Primicerius!' said old Candidus,
hoarsely, stepping forward, and respectfully
saluting his Commander. 'Give *me* that
task! I am old and tough and have grown
used to bloodshed; you are too young and
tender-hearted to witness this cruel work,
since every blow on us will be as a death-
wound to yourself from which yet you cannot
die! Be content to die the death—our
Master asks not of you a living Martyrdom!'

"'Thanks, old friend!' said Maurice, grasping the veteran's hand; 'but this is no self-sought pain! It belongeth to my office as head over this noble band, which is of God's appointment. You grant me my request?' he added, turning to the officer, who shrugged his shoulders, and moved away with a puzzled air.

"'Alas, alas!' muttered Candidus, falling back into his place, while tears gathered in his eyes for the first time for many a year. 'Would God I might die for thee, my son!'

"And Exuperius looked from one to another and said sadly to himself, 'I am not worthy! I am not worthy!'

"Then Maurice spoke for the last time on earth to the officers who had so often followed him into the thickest of the battle.

"'My brothers!' he said, 'the hour is come! Let us glorify God in our deaths as we have striven to glorify Him in our lives! Let us lay down our arms—emptying ourselves of earthly glory, even as He Who on Calvary suffered a shameful death for us. Let us kneel down and pray for our murderers, even as He also did, and as did the Blessed Stephen, he who first shed his blood for the Faith.'

" As he spoke he unbuckled his sword and helmet, and kneeling down laid them on the ground and folded his arms on his breast; the other officers followed his example, and joined him as he repeated the Lord's Prayer; and then in the silence that followed, his voice rose again alone,

" 'Lord, lay not this sin to their charge!' 'Father, forgive them, for they know not what they do!' 'Into Thy Hands we commend our spirit, for Thou hast redeemed us, O Lord Thou God of Truth!'

" 'O Primicerius!' said an anxious voice, 'pray for me that my faith fail not!'

" Maurice rose, and went quietly round to where the delicate-looking youth who had spoken knelt; but at that moment there was a commotion in the Imperial band, and one of the Tribunes, an officer higher in rank than the one commanding it, broke through and rode into the open space where the Christians knelt.

"'Why tarry ye?' he exclaimed, angrily. 'The Emperor's command is urgent, and brooks of no delay, and ye parley still with these Christian traitors! Upon them, men! let not one of them escape! And why art thou not prostrate as thy fellows before the power of Rome?' he added, seeing Maurice standing beside the trembling boy whom he was still encouraging by look and word—and as the young Commander faced him un-flinchingly with his clear untroubled eyes, he struck him with his sword-hilt a blow which laid him senseless on the ground.

"Then a great cry arose, and many of the Christians sprang up clutching their swords; but Candidus lifted up his voice and bade them back to their knees as their leader had desired, and they sank down again. Regulus uttered an oath and drove his spurs into his horse's flank as he saw the cowardly blow, and ere he had soothed it again there were flying hoofs on the mossy ground, and scattering the pagan soldiers right and left, Auster dashed once more up the hillock, and planted himself across his master's prostrate form.

"Ha! a noble steed!' exclaimed the Tribune. 'Lead him to my tent!' but as an attendant ran forward to obey his command, Regulus snatched a bow from one of the archers and sent an arrow straight to the charger's heart, and he fell dead beside his master.

"'Now God bless thee for that!' exclaimed Exuperius, whose clenched hands and livid face showed what it had cost *him* to lift no avenging hand. They were his last words. The enraged Tribune, who dared not quarrel with Regulus, turned upon him, and with one sweep of his sword struck off the proud young head, and thus he was

Death of St. Maurice.

spared the longer trial of patient forbearance which might have been beyond his strength. That blow was a signal for a general slaughter—the soldiers who had been hitherto held back by their centurion, mad with jealousy and superstitious terror and furious at the interruption to their revels, rushed upon their victims; only pausing for an instant at sight of him whom they had taken for a dead man, suddenly raising himself to his knees, and at sound of a clear ringing voice exclaiming,

"'Lo! I see the heavens opened!—Lord Jesus!'

"And, with the Holy Name yet on his lips, Maurice fell back with his head on Auster's neck, and died—suffering no second blow!"

"And Candidus, Uncle Max?" said Mabel, in an awestruck voice, after a pause, in which the pattering raindrops and the soft swaying of the wet leaves were the only sounds.

"Candidus was the first slain after the soldiers had shaken off their momentary panic at Maurice's dying strength.

" 'Ah, my sons!' he murmured, as he saw first one and then another of the two comrades who had been so dear to him, fall in their youthful vigour, 'beautiful and pleasant were ye in your lives and in death ye were not divided! May the Lord set me near ye in the army of Michael the Archangel; for I cannot think your work is done so soon. Nevertheless, O Lord, not my will but Thine be done!'

"And so *he*

> ' Bowed his neck, the death to feel.
> Who follows in his train ? ' "

And Uncle Max looked from one to another of his listeners.

" I don't think I could!" said Mabel, shuddering.

" You are not required to die for the faith now, my child," said her uncle, tenderly. " What you have to do is to *live* for it, and that you can and *will* do, I am sure, by trying in every little thing day by day to think first how you can best bring glory to God and good to every member of His Church, and so do your part towards *hastening the Coming of His glorious Kingdom.* That is what nerved these warrior-martyrs to take patiently, (and, as their foes might think, *cowardly*,) a shameful death, when they might have sold their lives very dear; and that same hope set before us must nerve *us* to fight the battle of life—taking patiently the little worries and disappointments, and doing bravely the little duties, and enjoying *thankfully* the little pleasures—of which our lives are made up."

" And what became of the rest of the Legion, Uncle Max ? " asked Mabel, presently. " Were any of them saved ? "

" The legend says that not one of them escaped the general massacre, little one ; but I cannot say for certain as to the truth of that. At all events, they made no resistance; and when the sun went down, the great hills cast their shadow over what seemed like a terrible battle-field, red with blood, and ghastly with corpses.

" I never pass through the village which stands on the scene of the martyrdom, and is called St. Maurice, in memory of it, without thinking of God's words to Moses : — ' Put off thy shoes from off thy feet, for the place whereon thou standest is holy ground [1] ! ' "

" Uncle Max, do you think we shall ever have another persecution ? " said Hugh, who had not spoken for some time, in a low voice.

" I do not know, Hugh. But I know that we need not *fear* even that, so long as we are trying to do our duty ' in that state of life unto which it hath pleased God to call us.' You know how a Church is built—with one stone after another fitted into its place, till at last it is so completely finished as to

[1] Exod. iii. 5.

be ready to bear on its summit the Cross which is its crown! And the little things I have been speaking of to Mabel are the stones which build up our lives, one after another, little by little, till unconsciously we are fitted (if we give ourselves up into our Builder's hand) to bear, if need be, even the golden Cross of Martyrdom."

There was silence again, and then Mabel said, " I have just done learning a hymn about what children may do for Jesus. It is the one we sang at the Children's Service last Sunday."

" Let us hear it!" said Uncle Max; and, sitting bolt upright on his knee, Mabel folded her hands, and repeated reverently : —

> " ' We are but little children weak,
>   Nor born in any high estate ;
>   What can we do for Jesus' sake
>   Who is so high and good and great?

> " ' We know the Holy Innocents
>   Laid down for Him their infant life,
>   And martyrs brave and patient saints
>   Have stood for Him in fire and strife.

" ' We wear the Cross they wore of old,
　　Our lips have learned like vows to make;
　　We need not die; we cannot fight;
　　What may we do for Jesus' sake?

" ' Oh! day by day each Christian child
　　Has much to do, without, within;
　　A death to die for Jesus' sake,
　　A weary war to wage with sin.

" ' When deep within our swelling hearts
　　The thoughts of pride and anger rise,
　　When bitter words are on our tongues,
　　And tears of passion in our eyes;

" ' Then we may stay the angry blow,
　　Then we may check the hasty word,
　　Give gentle answers back again,
　　And fight a battle for our Lord.

" ' With smiles of peace and looks of love,
　　Light in our dwellings we may make,
　　Bid kind good-humour brighten there,
　　And do all still for Jesus' sake.

" ' There's not a child so small and weak,
　　But has his little cross to take,
　　His little work of love and praise
　　That he may do for Jesus' sake. AMEN.' "

" Thank you, my child!" said her uncle,
when she had finished. "And have *you* anything for us to remember, Hugh?"

But Hugh shook his head, and it was not till Mabel had run out of the room to ask if her papa wanted to see Uncle Max before he went out, that he suddenly laid his head against his Uncle's shoulder, and whispered, "I think *you* have given *me* something to remember." Adding, with a jerk, "You know —about 'better is he that ruleth his spirit than he that taketh a city[1]!'"

"Exuperius' lesson, eh, lad? God grant you may learn it as well! The Holy Spirit is teaching it to you now, Hughie. Do not *disappoint* Him by refusing to practise it daily, that you may grow perfect in it!

"Now, good-bye. I must go and work in my Master's vineyard!"

And Uncle Max went his way, not hearing Hugh mutter, "I think you've been doing that all this time!"

[1] Prov. xvi. 32.

CLARENDON PRESS, OXFORD.
For the Society for Promoting Christian Knowledge.

PUBLICATIONS

Society for Promoting Christian Knowledge.

*Most of these Works may be had in ornamental bindings,
with gilt edges, at a small extra charge.*

Price
s. d.

AGNES AND KATIE IN SERVICE. A Sequel to
"Joy of Well Doing." 18mo. cloth boards . 1 0

A JOURNAL OF THE PLAGUE YEAR: being Observations, or Memorials, of the most Remarkable
Occurrences, as well Public as Private, which
happened in London during the last great
Visitation in 1665. Written by a Citizen who
continued all the while in London. To which
is added Some Account of the Great Fire in
1666. (Extracted from "Evelyn's Memoirs.")
Imp. 16mo., with 6 page Cuts on toned paper.
cloth boards 3 0

BRITISH BIRDS IN THEIR HAUNTS. By the Rev. .
C. A. Johns 10 0

CLEAR SHINING AFTER RAIN. (For Girls.) By
Mrs. Carey Brock. With 8 full-page Illustrations on toned paper. Crown 8vo. cloth boards 3 0

CYCLE OF LIFE, The. A Book of Poems for
Young and Old, Town and Country. Extra
cloth, gilt edges 7 6

DAVIE ARMSTRONG. A Story of the Fells. By
Austin Clare, Author of "André's Trials."
18mo. cloth boards 9

EARTH'S MANY VOICES. First and Second Series.
With illustrations on toned paper. Royal
16mo. extra cloth, gilt edges . . . each 2 0
The two series in one volume . . . 4 0

FAITHFUL AND TRUE; or, the Mother's Legacy.
(For Girls.) By E. J. Barnes. With 3 full-
page illustrations on toned paper. Crown 8vo.
cloth boards 1 6
[7. 11. 71].

Price
*. d.

FOUR SEASONS, The. Containing 40 plates, printed in colours, with descriptive Poetry. Royal 16mo. gilt edges 3 6

GROSSETESTE, BISHOP OF LINCOLN, The Life and Times of Robert. By George G. Perry, M.A. With 4 full-page Illustrations on toned paper. Post 8vo. cloth boards 2 6

HARRY WATERS AND JOHN HEARD. A Lesson from the Field; or, like Seed like Fruit. With four illustrations on toned paper. Crown 8vo. cloth boards 2 0

HARTZ BOYS, The; or, as a Man Sows, so must he Reap. With 1 full-page Illustration on toned paper. Crown 8vo. cloth boards . . 1 0

HELEN FREEMAN'S WORD. A Tale of Field Gang Life. 18mo. cloth boards . . . 1 0

HISTORY OF THE CRUSADERS, with four full-page engravings. By G. G. Perry, M.A. Fcp. 8vo. cloth boards, gilt edges 1 6

HUGH WYNFORD; or, the Cousin's Revenge. Fcp. 8vo. cloth boards 1 6

LAND OF ISRAEL, The: A Journey of Travels in Palestine, undertaken with special reference to its Physical Character. By H. B. Tristram, M.A., F.L.S. Second Edition. 8vo. cloth boards, with maps and coloured plates . . 21 0

LIFE IN THE WALLS, THE HEARTH, AND THE EAVES. With 4 full-page Illustrations. Printed on toned paper. Royal 16mo. cloth boards . 1 0

LIGHTHOUSE, The. (For Boys.) 18mo. cl. boards 1 0

MARION; or, the Smuggler's Wife. With 4 full-page Illustrations on toned paper. Crown 8vo. cloth boards 2 0

NATURAL HISTORY, Illustrated Sketches of. First and Second Series. Fcp. 8vo. cloth boards, each 2 6

Price
s. d.

NURSE MARGARET'S TWO ST. SYLVESTER EVES.
(For Girls.) A Tale. Translated from the
German by Ottilie Wildermuth. Royal 16mo   0   8

OCEAN, The. By P. H. Gosse, F.R.S. Post
8vo. cloth boards 4   6

OUR NATIVE SONGSTERS. By Anne Pratt. 73
coloured plates. Royal 16mo. cloth boards . 8   0

PENNY WISE AND POUND FOOLISH. By Mrs.
Carey Brock. Crown 8vo. cloth boards . . 2   0

PEOPLE OF EUROPE. First and Second Series in
a vol. 24 coloured plates. Royal 16mo. limp
cloth 2   6

RIGHT WAY AND THE WRONG WAY, The; or,
the Ardingley Lads. By A. R. N., Author of
"Woodbury Farm," "Margaret Vere," &c.
With 3 full-page Illustrations on toned paper.
Crown 8vo. cloth boards 1   6

RINA CLIFFE. (For Girls.) A Village Character.
By E. M. L. With 3 full-page Illustrations
on toned paper. Crown 8vo. cloth boards . 2   0

ROBINSON CRUSOE. New Edition. With four
page engravings. 12mo. cloth boards . . 2   6.

RUPERT OF THE RHINE. By Mary C. Bushe.
Fcp. 8vo. cloth boards 1   6

SCENES IN THE EAST. Consisting of twelve
coloured Photographic Views of Places mentioned in the Bible, beautifully executed, with
descriptive Letterpress. By the Rev. H. B.
Tristram, M.A., LL.D., F.R.S., &c., Author
of the "Land of Israel," &c. 4to. cloth
bevelled boards, gilt edges 7   6

SELBORNE, NATURAL HISTORY OF. By the late
Rev. Gilbert White, A.M. Arranged for
Young Persons. A new and revised Edition.
Post 8vo. cloth boards 3   9.

SINAI AND JERUSALEM; or, Scenes from Bible Lands. Consisting of coloured Photographic Views of Places mentioned in the Bible, including a Panoramic View of Jerusalem, with descriptive Letterpress. By the Rev. T. W. Holland, M.A., Hon. Sec. to the Palestine Exploration Fund. Demy 4to. cloth bevelled boards, gilt edges 7 6

SHIPWRECKS AND ADVENTURES AT SEA. Fcp. 8vo. cloth boards 2 0

TOM NEAL AND SARAH HIS WIFE, THE EXPERIENCES OF. Crown 8vo. cloth boards . . 1 6

TO SAN FRANCISCO AND BACK. By a London Parson. With numerous Illustrations. Crown 8vo. cloth boards 2 6

WANDERER, The. (For Boys.) By Mrs. Pearless (late Anne Pratt). Crown 8vo. with 3 full-page Illustrations, cloth boards . . . 2 0

WARM NESTS; or, Nellie Grange. (For Servants.) 18mo. cloth boards 1 0

WILD FLOWERS. By Anne Pratt. In two vols., containing 192 plates, printed in colours, 16mo. cloth boards 16 0

ZISKA: THE BLIND HERO OF BOHEMIA. A Sketch of the Hussite Reformation in the Fifteenth Century. With 1 full-page Illustration on toned paper. Crown 8vo. cloth boards . 1 0

Depositories:

77 GREAT QUEEN STREET, LINCOLN'S-INN FIELDS;
4 ROYAL EXCHANGE; 48 PICCADILLY;
AND BY ALL BOOKSELLERS.

CPSIA information can be obtained
at www.ICGtesting.com
Printed in the USA
BVHW061921120820
586213BV00003B/245